WHO AND WHEN?

The 17th CENTURY

Artists, Writers, and Composers

INTRODUCTION

The 17th century was a golden age for the arts. In England, William Shakespeare (*see page 74*) wrote some of his greatest plays, while in Italy, the composer Claudio Monteverdi (*see page 88*) pioneered a new musical form, the opera. To the north, Holland produced many of its greatest artists, headed by Rembrandt van Rijn and Jan Vermeer (*see pages 62 and 68*), while France could boast the most splendid court in Europe—the palace of Versailles. These achievements were all the more remarkable, given that they were created in a turbulent atmosphere of warfare and revolt.

Religion was a major cause of unrest. In the previous century, the call for reform had led to the foundation of the Protestant Church, which bitterly opposed the authority of Roman Catholicism. These tensions still divided Europe in the 1600s. The division lay at the heart of the Thirty Years' War, which affected much of the continent between 1618 and 1648. In England, meanwhile, the Civil War of 1642-49 was fueled by fears about the Catholic sympathies of King Charles I. And in France, hostility to the Protestant cause led to the cancellation of a law which had protected the Huguenots, or French Protestants, prompting many of them to flee the country.

The arts reflected these problems. The Protestant beliefs of English writers John Donne, a church minister famous for his sermons, and John Milton (*see pages 80 and 84*) shone through in their deeply religious works. In painting and architecture, meanwhile, Catholics used an exciting new style to help revive their faith. This style—the Baroque—was grand, theatrical, and emotional. The idea was to create buildings and pictures that would be as imposing as the great cathedrals and altarpieces of the Middle Ages, when the influence of Catholicism had been at its peak. Baroque artists sought to overwhelm, dazzle, and impress the viewer.

Baroque artists achieved these effects in various ways. The work of the Italian sculptor and architect Gianlorenzo Bernini (*see page 38*) shows the power and intensity which the Baroque could bring to religious art. Meanwhile, Peter Paul Rubens (*see page 14*) painted with great flamboyance and exuberance, overwhelming the viewer with color and energy. One of the favorite tricks of Baroque painters was to use dramatic contrasts between light and dark, or *chiaroscuro*. Like a spotlight on a stage, this helped to create a sense of theater. Caravaggio and Artemisia Gentileschi (*see pages 8 and 26*) were particularly fond of this device. Monteverdi's ornate musical compositions also have a Baroque feel.

The creation of large and impressive artworks was expensive. It could only be achieved because of Europe's growing wealth. Some of this came from increased trade and improved banking systems, but it was also due to the riches imported from foreign colonies. This trend had begun in the previous century, with Spanish and Portuguese exploits in South America. Now the world's leading colonial powers were the English, French, and Dutch. Holland's chief links were with the East Indies, while England and France looked to North America. In 1607, the English established a colony in Virginia. And in 1620, the Pilgrim Fathers, who had sailed across in the *Mayflower*, established a new settlement at Plymouth, Massachusetts. By the 1630s, expeditions from Europe were commonplace.

The spread of wealth encouraged the development of new art forms. In Holland, for example, the middle classes became rich, and wanted a different kind of picture to spend their money on. In place of the large religious or historical works designed for churches or palaces, these new patrons wanted smaller paintings to decorate their own homes. Views of everyday life, landscapes, and pictures of flowers or fruit became the most popular themes. And as the group portraits of Frans Hals and Rembrandt van Rijn (*see pages 20 and 62*) show, they also liked to have pictures of themselves, dressed in the impressive uniforms that went with their jobs.

There was still a demand for royal painters of high quality. Painters like Anthony Van Dyck and Diego Velázquez (*see pages 44 and 50*) portrayed the monarchs of England and Spain in all their splendor. But the most glorious of the European courts was in France—King Louis XIV's palace of Versailles, near Paris. During his reign, Louis surrounded himself with such treasures that he became known as the "Sun King." In the arts, he promoted Classicism, seen in the mythological paintings of Nicolas Poussin and the landscapes of Claude Lorrain (*see pages 32 and 56*). This style looked back to the classical art of ancient Greece and Rome. For Louis, this was a welcome association: These civilizations conjured up images of military strength, imperial grandeur, and political stability.

CARAVAGGIO

A highly original painter, Caravaggio was as famous for his unconventional life as for his revolutionary use of light and shade, and stark realism in painting. He was the most influential Italian painter of the 17th century.

The painter who became famous as Caravaggio was born near Bergamo, in northern Italy, in 1573. He was christened Michelangelo Merisi, but he later gave himself the name of his home village—Caravaggio.

EARLY LIFE
When he was 12, Caravaggio became an apprentice, or trainee, at the studio of the artist Simone Peterzano, in Milan. Little else is known about his early life, except that his mother died in 1590, and two years later he, his brother, and his sister divided the family property between them. His share enabled the young artist to set off for Rome, the Italian capital, in about 1592. Artists had a better chance of finding work there, by gaining commissions from the Roman Catholic Church.

By this time, Caravaggio was very poor; he had spent his inheritance quickly and unwisely. Then, he got a job with Giuseppe Cesari d'Arpino, a successful artist known for his frescoes,

a type of wall painting. This was a promising job, since Cesari had several church commissions. But the arrangement came to an end when Caravaggio was kicked by a horse and had to go to the hospital.

POWERFUL STILL LIFES
At this time, Caravaggio was producing small domestic scenes and "still-life" pictures—studies of flowers, fruit, and everyday objects. Still-life painting had been unfashionable for a long time, but Caravaggio revived it as an art form. He said that it "took as much skill to paint a good picture of flowers as of figures."

Only one of Caravaggio's still-life compositions has survived, dating from about 1598. This picture shows the artist bringing a startling new realism to still-life painting: the fruit in the picture is not perfectly shaped and

David with the Head of Goliath (detail), c.1605-06, by Caravaggio
This bleeding head of the dead Goliath is said to be a self-portrait of the artist.

The Supper at Emmaus, c.1601, by Caravaggio
This striking painting, lit by a stark white light, shows Christ appearing to his disciples after his Resurrection. Caravaggio chooses to show the moment of realization: "Then their eyes were opened and they recognized Him" (Luke 24:31). Cleophas, on the left, pushes back his chair in astonishment, while the second disciple flings out his arms.

hated anything that was false or artificially pretty in art, which is why he painted many of his figures with wrinkled peasant faces and dirty feet. He wanted to show real people, in a way that his audience could relate to. This was in stark contrast to the stale, dignified figures of saints of centuries of official Church art.

A NEW BRUTALITY

Compared to the graceful power of masterpieces by High Renaissance masters like Michelangelo and Raphael, Caravaggio's realism appeared vulgar, rude, and brutally down to earth. He would often find, therefore, that priests rejected his religious commissions.

The rawness of Caravaggio's painting reflected his own violent and restless nature. He was arrested more than once during his lifetime and accused of several different crimes. His offenses included attacking another painter with a stick, carrying a sword and a dagger without permission, throwing a dish of hot artichokes at a waiter, and attacking a lawyer because he had flirted with Caravaggio's girlfriend.

The Dutch art historian Karel van Mander described the artist's volatile personality in 1603: "He does not study his art constantly, so that after two weeks of work he will sally forth for two months with his rapier [sword] at his side … going from one tennis court to another, always ready to argue or fight, so that he is impossible to get along with."

Caravaggio's behavior finally brought tragedy. On May 28, 1606, he played tennis against a man named Ranuccio

---

"Without the aid of God or man … he died, as miserably as he had lived." (contemporary artist, Giovanni Baglione)

Tommasoni. Afterward, a fight broke out over a bet they had made and Caravaggio killed Tommasoni. He had to go on the run.

The artist took refuge in Naples for a year, hoping that his friends in Rome would convince the pope to pardon him. When this did not happen, he left for the island of Malta, south of Sicily. Here he won a major commission from a religious order, the Knights of Malta.

Caravaggio painted his largest work for the Knights in 1608. It was *The Beheading of St. John the Baptist*, in honor of the order's patron saint. The knights were so impressed that they made the artist a Knight of the Order of Obedience. But the fiery Caravaggio later quarreled with one of the knights and had to escape once more, to Syracuse in Sicily, and then to Naples, in southern Italy.

MAJOR WORKS

c.1595	YOUNG MAN AS BACCHUS
c.1597	MEDUSA
1599-1600	THE MARTYRDOM OF ST. MATTHEW; THE CALLING OF ST. MATTHEW
1600-01	THE CONVERSION OF ST. PAUL; THE CRUCIFIXION OF ST. PETER
c.1601	THE SUPPER AT EMMAUS
1606	THE DEATH OF THE VIRGIN
1608	THE BEHEADING OF ST. JOHN THE BAPTIST

Caravaggio's friends in Rome were still trying to get him a pardon from the pope. After four years of restlessness, the artist was desperate to return to the Holy City. In the summer of 1610, he left Naples by ship and landed at Port' Ercole, 80 miles north of Rome. By a twist of fate, he was mistaken for someone else, and arrested on shore. He was held for two days in prison.

A DRAMATIC END

By the time he was released, his ship had left with his belongings. According to Baglione, he was furious, and ran along the beach to try to catch sight of the ship, but collapsed in the summer heat. He died of a "raging fever" shortly afterward, on July 18, 1610. He was not even 40 years old. The pardon he had longed for was granted—but it had come too late.

PETER PAUL RUBENS

The greatest Flemish artist of the 17th century, Rubens enjoyed a brilliantly successful career, not just in art but also in international diplomacy. His work brims with color, enthusiasm, and his zest for life.

Peter Paul Rubens was born on June 28, 1577, in Siegen, Germany. His lawyer father, Jan, had left his native Antwerp nine years earlier to escape religious persecution. Today, Antwerp is in Belgium, but at this time it was in Flanders, which was part of a larger area ruled by the king of Spain, and known as the Spanish Netherlands. In 1587, Jan died, and the family moved back to Antwerp, where Rubens's mother had wealthy relatives.

AN EARLY TRAINING

Peter Paul had a good education, but the family was short of money, so when he was 13 he took a job as a page in a noble household. There he gained a familiarity with aristocratic life that would be useful in later years, when he would mix with royalty.

Rubens did not work as a page for long, however; he had already decided that he wanted to be an artist. His mother arranged for him to study with Tobias Verhaecht, a distant relative.

Rubens soon moved on to study with Adam van Noort, later completing his training with Otto van Veen.

All three of Rubens's masters are now regarded as very minor artists. Van Veen, however, was a cultured man. He had spent several years in Italy; his enthusiasm for the country and its art probably inspired Rubens to see it for himself. Rubens qualified as a master in the Antwerp painters' guild in 1598, at the age of 20. Then, after two more years working with van Veen, he set out for Italy. This would be his base for the next eight years.

At first, the young artist went to Venice, in the north of the country. There, he impressed an employee of Vincenzo Gonzaga, the duke of Mantua, with his sketches. The duke was equally impressed and at once took Rubens into his service. This gave him a wonderful

Rubens and Isabella Brant, 1609-10, by Peter Paul Rubens
This tender portrait shows the artist and his first wife shortly after their wedding.

opportunity to complete his artistic education. Vincenzo was a great art-lover, and he sent Rubens to leading centers of Italian art, such as Florence and Rome, to make copies of famous paintings for his collection.

A SKILL FOR DIPLOMACY

In 1603, the duke entrusted Rubens with his first diplomatic mission, taking gifts to Philip III of Spain. These included two paintings that were damaged by rain on the journey. Rubens demonstrated his skill and presence of mind by painting superb copies of the originals, which greatly impressed the Spanish royal family.

By 1604, Rubens was back in Italy, where he had a growing reputation and good contacts. In 1606, he won a prestigious commission to paint the altarpiece for a new church, known as Chiesa Nuova, in Rome, where he was now living. In the city, Rubens studied ancient art, and the work of Renaissance masters such as Michelangelo.

RETURN TO ANTWERP

Rubens was very happy in Italy, and probably intended to stay in the country for the rest of his life. But in October 1608, he received news that his mother was very ill. He traveled to Antwerp at once, but his mother was already dead by the time he arrived.

Rubens wanted to return to Italy, but he was persuaded to stay in Flanders. The Archduke Albert and his wife, the Infanta Isabella, who ruled the area on behalf of the king of Spain, appointed him court painter in 1609. The artist

MARIE DE' MEDICI

Rubens's most ambitious project illustrated the life of an Italian princess who became queen of France.

Between 1622 and 1625, Rubens produced a series of 25 paintings for the mother of King Louis XIII of France, Marie de' Medici (*right*). Rubens made this informal and sensitive drawing as a study for the cycle. It is far more realistic than the finished paintings, which flattered Marie's ageing features.

Marie, who had ruled France as queen regent between 1610 and 1614, commissioned these paintings to decorate her new palace in Paris. She had a great love of art. The series was one of Rubens's greatest achievements. Although Marie was, in fact, an unappealing figure,

only agreed to accept the position on the condition that he did not have to live at his employer's court in Brussels.

In the same year, Rubens married Isabella Brant, the 17-year-old daughter of an Antwerp lawyer. The marriage was very happy and the couple would have four children together. In 1610, Rubens put down further roots when he bought some land in Antwerp on which

Rubens portrays the trivial events of her life with great splendor. He blended imagination, history, allegory, and portraiture to create a glorious tribute to the queen mother. In one of the paintings, for example, Rubens portrays Marie as Protector of the Arts, while in another, she is tutored by Minerva, goddess of wisdom.

he built a magnificent Italian-style palace. The following year, his first child, Clara Serena, was born.

Over the next few years, Rubens established his reputation as the leading painter in northern Europe. Two of his greatest masterpieces were the huge altarpieces of the *Raising of the Cross* and the *Descent from the Cross*. These works were striking examples of the painter's use of drama, energy, and vivid color. These qualities helped make him one of the leading exponents of the Baroque, a 17th-century style of art that aimed to overwhelm its viewer by a direct appeal to the senses or emotions.

A PROLIFIC WORKER

Commissions flooded into Rubens's studio, which was unequaled in Europe for its output. He produced scores of religious works for churches and abbeys. He could cope with them all only because of his formidable energy

> "My talents are such that I have never lacked courage to undertake any design, however vast in size."
> (Peter Paul Rubens)

and his remarkable powers of organization. He worked long hours. He rose at 4:00 A.M. every day to go to Mass, being a devout Catholic.

Yet even Rubens could not carry out all the work on his own. He therefore employed assistants, who carried out much of the physical act of painting between the design and the master's finishing touches. Demand to join his studio was very great, and many of Antwerp's leading painters of the time worked there at some stage, including Anthony Van Dyck (*see page 44*).

The Garden of Love, 1632-34, by Peter Paul Rubens
This picture typically shows Rubens's love of life's pleasures. Happy lovers enjoy themselves in a fantasy landscape, while cupids, or gods of love, fly excitedly around.

Great commissions came from abroad, too. Rubens's patrons included some of the most prominent figures in Europe, including Marie de' Medici, the mother of King Louis XIII of France. In 1621, Marie invited Rubens to France and commissioned a series of 25 large pictures illustrating her life for her new palace in Paris. As well as painting pictures on a wide range of subjects, Rubens also turned his hand to various types of design work, including several tapestries and title pages of books.

Perhaps the best-known feature of Rubens's art is his voluptuous female nudes, his ideal of feminine beauty. Plump proportions appealed to him both as a man and as an artist. Curvy, fleshy women were in fashion, and were also interesting to paint.

In 1626, Rubens's beloved wife Isabella died. Although deeply upset, Rubens was not a man to brood and he directed his energies not just into painting, but once again into diplomacy. He put his linguistic skills to good use in this role. As well as his native Flemish and perfect Italian, he was also fluent in French, German, Spanish, and Latin, which at the time was the international language.

FURTHER TRAVELS

After the death of Archduke Albert in 1621, Rubens became a trusted adviser to his widow, the Infanta Isabella. In 1628, he traveled as her diplomatic representative to Spain, where he charmed King Philip IV and became a friend of his court painter, Diego Velázquez (*see page 50*).

This journey led in turn to Rubens going to England on behalf of Philip in 1629 and 1630. There, Rubens helped to negotiate a peace treaty between England and Spain. The art-loving English king, Charles I, knighted Rubens and also commissioned a series of paintings from him. Rubens painted these in Antwerp, and sent them to England in 1635.

In 1630, at the age of 53, Rubens remarried. His bride, Hélène Fourment, was the 16-year-old daughter of a rich silk merchant, and the niece of Rubens's first wife. She bore him five more children. The artist now began to give up his diplomatic duties to devote more time to his family and his painting, which he described as *la dolcissima professione* or the "sweetest of professions." His love of both his wives and his children shines through the paintings and drawings he did of them.

In 1635, Rubens bought a splendid country house, the Het Steen, or "Stone House." Living in the country inspired a new passion for landscape painting. He still worked hard in his Antwerp studio, however, for the demand for his works was unceasing.

In his final years, Rubens's right arm was often crippled with gout, making it impossible for him to paint. His health continued to deteriorate, and he died in Antwerp on May 30, 1640, at the age of

---

"In no branch of the art is Rubens greater than in landscape." (19th-century artist, John Constable)

---

62. His death was mourned throughout Europe, for he was regarded not only as a superb artist, but also as one of the greatest men of his time, admired by virtually everyone who met him.

MAJOR WORKS

1610-11	RAISING OF THE CROSS
1611-14	DESCENT FROM THE CROSS
1622-25	MARIE DE' MEDICI CYCLE
c.1625	THE STRAW HAT
1632-34	THE GARDEN OF LOVE
c.1636	AUTUMN LANDSCAPE WITH VIEW OF HET STEEN
1639	THE THREE GRACES

FRANS HALS

One of the greatest portrait painters of the 17th century, Frans Hals created informal and relaxed images of the people around him. Yet although he was successful, he lived most of his life in poverty.

Frans Hals was born in 1582 or 1583 in Antwerp, the son of Franchoys Hals, a weaver. Antwerp was a prosperous trading city in Flanders, in the south of the Spanish Netherlands. During Hals's lifetime, the northern part of these territories broke away from Spain and eventually became known as the Dutch Republic.

FIRST STEPS
We do not know exactly when the Hals family left Antwerp, but by 1591 they had settled in Haarlem, where Franchoys could find work in the busy textile industry. We know little about Hals's early career. One suggestion is that he studied with Karel van Mander, one of Haarlem's leading painters, who also later wrote a book of artists' lives.

In 1610, Hals became a member of the Haarlem Guild of St. Luke, the city's association of artists. This allowed him to set up an independent workshop, and to take on apprentices. At about the same time as this, he married

Anneke Harmansdr. The couple had three children. Two of the children died in infancy and Anneke herself died in 1615. She was buried in a pauper's, or poor person's, grave—Hals would suffer severe financial difficulties throughout his life.

Only a few paintings by Hals are known up to this point, and they are not very good. If he had died at the same time as Anneke, his name might have been forgotten. In 1617, he married again. His second wife was Lysbeth Reyniersdr, a peasant woman with a quarrelsome temper, who often got into trouble for brawling.

A MAJOR BREAKTHROUGH
In 1616, Hals began his first major work, a group portrait of the *Banquet of the Officers of the St. George Civic Guard Company*. The company was a citizen

Possible self-portrait, after Frans Hals
This is thought to be a later copy of a painting by Hals. The artist and date of the work are both unknown.

army set up to counter the threat of invasion from Spain. As the Dutch Republic grew stronger, and it seemed less likely that Spain would invade, the company became more of a social than a military group.

Hals himself was a member of the St. George company. His familiarity with his comrades may have helped him to

> "His paintings are imbued with such ... vitality that he seems to defy nature herself."
> (a 17th-century writer)

capture the spirit and friendship among the officers. The picture made Hals's reputation—no other artist before him had created such a feeling of liveliness and character in this kind of group portrait. He became known as a leading painter of life-size group portraits. He painted ten further similar pictures throughout his career—more than any other Dutch painter of the time.

MONEY TROUBLES

Despite his success, Hals was always short of money. Sometimes he dealt in pictures or restored old paintings to help make ends meet. In 1616, he was taken to court for not paying maintenance for the children of his first marriage. Early in the 1630s, he was

INFORMAL POSES

In his portraits, Hals often made people look as if they had been caught in a passing moment.

Painting someone's portrait is a long process, but the people in Hals's pictures never look as if they have been sitting patiently for hours, waiting for the artist to finish. Sometimes, they lounge casually (*above right*), or have an arm over the back of a chair, as if they have just turned to face us as we enter the room.

Many of his portraits include the sitter's hands, and he had several different ways of painting them. Often, he shows a sitter holding a hat or gloves, or some other object such as a book. Sometimes, the sitter poses with one hand resting casually on a hip. He also sometimes shows

sued by both his landlord and his shoemaker, and in 1654, a baker seized his property because of an unpaid bill. The goods Hals handed over were pitifully meager.

A major reason for Hals's money problems must have been his growing family. Lysbeth and he had at least eight children. They all brought their parents particular worries. In 1642, the couple's

the sitter with arms spread so that the elbows point out toward us from the picture.

Almost all of Hals's 300 or so surviving paintings are portraits, but he was so fluent and imaginative that he rarely repeated a pose exactly. He could always find something new to say.

Hals does not appear to have flattered or idealized his sitters by improving their features. Instead, he seems to have shown them exactly as they were, with all their individual peculiarities. It is this that enables us to identify with his sitters as real personalities.

daughter Sara became pregnant with her second child, and later that year their son Pieter, who was mentally ill, was locked up because he was thought to be a public danger.

AN INDEPENDENT SPIRIT

Hals's rebellious spirit was another thing that stood in the way of his earning a good living. In 1636, at a time when he desperately needed money, he refused to complete a portrait of Amsterdam civic guards that would have earned him a large sum. Hals was unwilling to make the short journey to Amsterdam to finish the painting, and it was completed by another artist.

Despite his attitude toward patrons, Hals was at the height of his popularity at this time. In addition to his civic guard groups, he also painted many single and double portraits of both men and women.

The Dutch Republic was quickly becoming the dominant trading power in Europe, and there were plenty of wealthy citizens who wanted to show their pride in their achievements by having their portrait painted. Hals rarely painted anything other than portraits. Even his occasional religious subjects and scenes of everyday life have a portraitlike character.

A UNIQUE STYLE

Hals's great gift as a portraitist was his ability to capture a sense of lively movement and expression, making the work of many of his predecessors seem stiff by comparison. The sense of something having just happened or being about to happen in his pictures seems to have reflected the way he worked in his studio.

Not one of his drawings has survived, so far as we know. He probably worked directly onto the canvas without the elaborate preparations used by many painters. If you examine his pictures, you can see that he must have used the paintbrush quickly and vigorously. The

ARTEMISIA GENTILESCHI

Artemisia Gentileschi was one of the very few successful women artists of the 17th century. Many of her paintings take a fresh, bold, and highly dramatic look at the lives of famous Biblical heroines.

The determined and uncompromising artist Artemisia Gentileschi was born in Rome, in central Italy, on or just before July 8, 1593, the day of her baptism. Her father, Orazio, was a talented painter who mainly produced religious works. Her mother, Prudentia, died when Artemisia was 12 years old. There were four other children in the family, all boys.

Gentileschi probably had little education, because at this time the only girls who received formal tuition were daughters of the aristocracy. When she was 19, she claimed that she could read only a little, but several letters survive in her own handwriting from later in her life. She must have learned to read and write as an adult.

From an early age, however, Gentileschi was exposed to the world of art, since her father mixed with some of the most famous artists of the day. Those who came from northern Europe to study in Rome usually settled in the quarter where her family lived.

At first, Gentileschi's father, Orazio, probably taught Artemisia the basics of painting himself. Then, she studied under Orazio's assistant, Agostino Tassi. One of her brothers also trained as a painter, but he was not very good at it. Artemisia, on the other hand, showed a natural talent. This made Orazio very proud; he would always remain one of Artemisia's greatest admirers. Father and daughter did not conform to the stereotypes about men and women. Orazio's work is graceful and elegant—more "feminine"—while Artemisia's is powerful, strong, and vigorous—much more "masculine."

THE GREAT CARAVAGGIO

Orazio was a friend of Caravaggio's (*see page 8*), the Italian painter who shocked the art world with his dramatic use of light and shade and his down-to-earth

Self-portrait as the Allegory of Painting, c.1635, by Artemisia Gentileschi
The artist celebrates her craft—painting—in this striking portrait.

treatment of serious religious subjects. Caravaggio's work had a strong influence on the young Artemisia. She understood the emotional power of the master's work.

COURT SCANDAL

In 1612, when Gentileschi was 18, she was involved in a court case after she accused Agostino Tassi, her painting tutor, of attacking her. To prove her truthfulness to the court, she was

> "There is nothing in the history of painting to prepare us for Gentileschi's expression of female physical power."
> (a 20th-century art historian)

tortured with thumbscrews. But, even though the assault almost certainly took place, Tassi was acquitted after a group of his friends testified on his behalf. They claimed that he had a spotless character, and that Gentileschi had provoked him. The experience of the attack and the long trial must have had a lasting effect on Gentileschi.

SUCCESS IN FLORENCE

On November 29, 1612, a month after the end of the court case, Gentileschi married Pietro Stiattesi, a Florentine

INSPIRED BY JUDITH

Gentileschi drew great inspiration from the story of the Jewish heroine, Judith.

The story of Judith (right) appears in the Book of Judith. It is included in the Vulgate—the Roman Catholic Bible, written in Latin—but in Protestant Bibles it is printed in the "Apocrypha," an appendix of additional books. It tells how Judith, a beautiful Jewish woman, single-handedly defeated the Assyrian army which was attacking the Jews. She went into the enemy camp, distracted the Assyrian general Holofernes, encouraged him, and then cut off his head.

Gentileschi painted a number of different versions of the story throughout her career, sometimes showing Judith with her

painter. She moved with him from Rome to Florence, where her career soon flourished. Her husband's connections no doubt helped her to find work, but her continued success depended entirely on her own talent.

She showed great strength of character in competing in a man's world, for even the best women painters at this time were generally regarded

maidservant. She emphasized the women's physical strength.

Gentileschi admired strong women, especially those who stood up for themselves and their beliefs. She also applied these principles to her own life. She was determined to be a successful artist, despite the fact that most painters at that time were men.

as curiosities rather than serious artists. Gentileschi set her sights high. Instead of traditional women's subjects, such as small-scale portraits and still lifes of plants and fruit, she excelled at large-scale religious works—one of the most highly regarded kinds of paintings.

Her reputation grew rapidly. She became known as "that famous artist," and moved in the highest circles. At the age of just 23, in 1616, she was made an official member of the academy of painters in Florence—the first woman ever to have received the honor.

In 1617, she was hired to take part in a tribute to Michelangelo, the famous Italian Renaissance painter and sculptor. Michelangelo's great-nephew had bought a villa in Florence and named it the Casa Buonarroti for the painter's family name. He asked Gentileschi to be one of the artists to decorate it. It was a very important commission. She painted *The Allegory of the Inclination* for the ceiling of one of the villa's main rooms. Her patron paid her a higher fee than some of the male artists working on the project.

RETURN TO ROME

In around 1618, Gentileschi and her husband had a daughter, whom they named Prudentia for Gentileschi's mother. But the couple separated soon afterward, and eventually completely lost touch. In 1620, she left Florence, and after visiting Genoa and Venice, she returned to her native Rome. Her patrons in Florence had included members of the powerful Medici family, and in Rome she worked for equally important people, notably cardinals Antonio and Francesco Barberini, nephews of the pope, Urban VIII.

GENTILESCHI'S HEROINES

In Rome, Gentileschi painted *Judith with Her Maidservant*, one of many images she produced of the Jewish heroine, Judith. At other times, she produced visions of other women from

Judith with Her Maidservant, c.1618, by Artemisia Gentileschi
Gentileschi painted several versions of the story of Judith. Here, the startled heroine and accomplice turn toward a suspicious sight or sound after having killed Holofernes.

the Bible, such as Esther, a Jewish woman who persuaded the Persian king Ahasuerus not to slaughter the Jews, and Susanna, a beautiful woman who resisted the advances of two Jewish tribal elders. Gentileschi's pictures stressed the strength and determination of the women.

In about 1630, Gentileschi, by now a celebrity, moved to Naples. At the time, it was the largest and most important city in Italy. It was under the control of the Spanish empire, and was an important port for trade on the Mediterranean Sea. Because of its many wealthy inhabitants, it was a good place for artists to look for work. This must have been one reason why Gentileschi moved there. Otherwise, she hated the city, "because of the fighting, the hard life, and the high cost of living."

Naples, however, offered a natural home for Gentileschi's vigorous and passionate style. At the beginning of the 17th century, Caravaggio had worked in the city, and had inspired local artists. His style was still very popular there in the 1630s, although it had gone out of fashion in Rome.

The painters who still followed Caravaggio were known as the Caravaggisti. Because Gentileschi's work was partly inspired by Caravaggio, and similar in some ways to his art, the Caravaggisti in Naples welcomed her to the city. Gentileschi's patrons there included Maria of Austria, who was the sister of the king of Spain.

WORK IN ENGLAND

In 1638, Gentileschi traveled to England at the request of King Charles I. She joined her father, who was working on one of the royal houses just south of London. Her father had been court painter to Charles since 1626, but he was now in very bad health, which may have been the reason for her visit. Her father died in 1639, but Gentileschi remained in London until 1641. She painted numerous pictures for several royal houses and palaces.

LAST YEARS IN NAPLES

Gentileschi returned to Naples in 1642, and seems to have spent the rest of her life there. We know little about her last

> "In the profession of painting ... she has no peer."
> (Orazio Gentileschi)

years, apart from the fact that she suffered poverty and poor health.

The date of her death is unknown, but it was in either 1652 or 1653, when she was around 60 years old. Although her fame declined after her death, in the 20th century she has been rediscovered and hailed as a great artist.

MAJOR WORKS

1610	SUSANNA AND THE ELDERS
c.1618	JUDITH WITH HER MAIDSERVANT
c.1620	JUDITH DECAPITATING HOLOFERNES
1623	ESTHER BEFORE AHASUERUS
c.1635	SELF-PORTRAIT AS THE ALLEGORY OF PAINTING

NICOLAS POUSSIN

Poussin's passion for the works of antiquity led him from his native France to Rome, where he lived for most of his life. There he produced paintings which were to shape French art for the next two centuries.

Nicolas Poussin was born in June 1594 in Les Andelys, a small town in northern France. His parents were from the minor nobility, although by the time of Poussin's birth, they were very poor. Nicolas received only a simple education, but he studied Latin—an important foundation for his later interest in classical antiquity.

INSPIRED TO PAINT

Poussin would have had little opportunity to study paintings in his home environment. His interest in art was sparked off by an outside influence. In 1611, a painter called Quentin Varin came to Les Andelys to paint three pictures for the local church. Varin was an unexceptional artist, but his paintings filled Poussin with enthusiasm.

Encouraged by Varin, Poussin decided to go to Paris to train as an artist. His parents were against the idea, but in 1612, the 18-year-old secretly left home.

Poussin soon arrived in Paris, where he would stay for the following 12 years. He trained under two minor artists, Ferdinand Elle and Georges Lallemand. More importantly, he gained access to the royal art collection. There he could see classical Roman sculpture and paintings by the greatest masters of the Italian Renaissance. These works inspired him to travel to Rome.

TRAINING IN PARIS

He could not afford to make the journey right away, however. He found work only occasionally, and as a result was always short of money. In 1622, he painted six paintings for the Jesuit church in Paris. Shortly afterward, Poussin produced a series of drawings illustrating scenes from the Roman poet Ovid's great work, *Metamorphoses*.

Finally, in 1624, he had saved the money to make the journey. Although he was almost 30 years old, he regarded

Self-portrait, 1630, by Nicolas Poussin
Poussin drew this self-portrait at the age of 36, while he was convalescing from a serious illness.

Holy Family on the Steps, 1648, by Nicolas Poussin
In this calm and monumental work, the Madonna holds the baby Jesus, who reaches out for an apple—a symbol of life—offered to him by St. John. This painting displays the principles on which Poussin based his work—clarity, simplicity, and order.

local French artists resented this "outsider" having such an important job. He became the target of petty jealousies, a situation which was not improved by the sharpness of his own tongue. Just two years later, in 1642, Poussin returned to Rome for good. He summarized his stay in Paris as a journey from paradise into hell.

MAKING CONTACTS

The time in France was not entirely wasted, however. Poussin enlarged his circle of patrons. Most of these men were bankers and civil servants, rather than noblemen and royalty, and they were largely content to let Poussin choose his own compositions. This enabled him to withdraw from public commissions and work alone in his studio. The next decade was his busiest and most fruitful period.

CAREFUL PLANNING

In planning any new work, Poussin would first research his subject thoroughly. He would carefully read the story he was about to illustrate, which he usually found in the Bible or in the works of ancient Greek and Roman writers such as Plutarch and Livy. He then made sketches in pen and wash.

During this time, Poussin's style reached a peak of classical grandeur. He produced pure geometric compositions, portraying his subjects clearly, without any distracting elements. He toned down his interest in sensuous color, and concentrated on the serious subject

> "A mind thrown back 2,000 years and ... naturalized in antiquity."
> (18th-century artist, Joshua Reynolds)

matter. His figures often seem frozen, like statues in heroic poses. Poussin worked slowly and carefully to achieve this effect.

MAKING MODELS
First, he drew sketches of his ideas. Then, he made small wax models and placed them in a box like a tiny theater, so he could judge effects of light. Next he made larger models to capture the precise gestures he required. He also added thin taffeta or wet paper to the models, to lend the impression of drapery. Only then would he start work on the canvas itself.

The use of wax models was not new—artists had used them in the 16th century. But it was an extremely slow and laborious process. Poussin consid-

ered himself lucky if he completed painting a single head in a day's work. It is not surprising, therefore, that when someone asked the secret of his success, Poussin replied that it was "because he neglected nothing."

In Poussin's later years, landscape played an important role in his art. Between 1660 and 1664, he painted a series of pictures called *The Four Seasons*. The series showed not only the different times of the year, but also the times of the day, the ages of life, and the spiritual history of humanity.

SHAPING THE FUTURE
In old age, Poussin's powers as an artist deserted him. For years he had suffered from trembling hands, but in 1664, he was partly paralyzed, and could no longer work. He died in Rome the following year, aged 71. But the influence of his austere, classical works lived on for centuries, shaping official teaching of art in France, and inspiring generations of French artists.

MAJOR WORKS

1627	THE DEATH OF GERMANICUS
1628	THE MARTYRDOM OF ST. ERASMUS
1635-36	TRIUMPH OF PAN
c.1637	ET IN ARCADIA EGO
1648	HOLY FAMILY ON THE STEPS
1660-64	THE FOUR SEASONS

GIANLORENZO BERNINI

A dynamic sculptor and architect, Bernini was a major figure in the growth of the Baroque— a lively style of art with a powerful emotional impact. He filled all his works with great energy and drama.

Gianlorenzo Bernini was born in Naples, a city on the coast south of Rome, in 1598. From an early age he was taught by his father, a successful sculptor, who was asked to work for the pope. The family, therefore, moved to live in Rome in 1604, when Gianlorenzo was six.

A YOUNG GENIUS

Gianlorenzo inherited his father's ability to portray changing human emotions in sculpture. He studied the art of ancient Greece, and copied works from the pope's own collection with extraordinary skill. Many people even mistook a marble carving that he did in his teens, the *Goat Amalthea*, for a genuine classical work from antiquity.

Bernini began working on his own projects from about the age of 19. He carved several busts—head-and-shoulder portraits in marble—of cardinals, or leading priests. These show his extraordinary ability to make cold stone look like living, breathing flesh.

Before he began carving, Bernini would always draw his subjects as they went about their business. By doing so, he got to know the person's moods, feelings, and expressions. This helps to explain why his portrait busts seem as lively and spontaneous as a photographer's snapshots.

Bernini went to great lengths to make his faces and figures seem real and alive. According to legend, to achieve a sensation of horror in his sculpture, the *Damned Soul*, he studied his own face while holding his leg in a fire. The face he carved is screwed up in agony, and is terrifying to look at.

Bernini soon came to the notice of the art-loving Cardinal Scipione Borghese. The artist sculpted one of his most famous pieces, *Apollo and Daphne*, for Borghese between 1622 and 1625. In ancient Greek myth, the

Self-portrait, 1630,
by Gianlorenzo Bernini
This somber, yet dignified, painting shows the sculptor at the age of 32.

nymph Daphne was pursued by the sun god, Apollo. As Apollo was about to catch her, Daphne's father, the river god, changed her into a tree. Bernini chose to show the dramatic moment of Daphne's escape, as her arms sprout leaves and her feet are rooted to the ground.

HONORS AND ADMIRATION

Thanks to his powerful patrons and his own abilities, Bernini began winning honors when he was in his early twenties. The pope knighted him, and he became head of the main art school in Rome, the Academy of St. Luke.

In 1623, one of his patrons, Cardinal Maffeo Barberini, became pope, taking the name Urban VIII. The new pope was ambitious, and an admirer of Bernini. He compared the young sculptor with the 16th-century master Michelangelo.

Urban wanted Bernini to work as both an architect and a sculptor, as Michelangelo had. Bernini responded in his own energetic way, designing churches, monuments, and fountains. He also added towers to the central church of the Roman Catholic faith, the basilica of St. Peter's in Rome.

In the church lies the tomb of St. Peter, which is supposed to contain the body of Jesus' disciple. In 1624, Bernini designed a 93-foot-high canopy, or *baldacchino*, over the tomb. It would take him nearly ten years to complete. His design involved huge twisted columns. The whole canopy was cast in bronze, using metal taken from the ancient Roman building, the Pantheon.

Many people in Rome were horrified that this ancient relic was being dis-

THE BAROQUE

Baroque sculptors, painters, and architects aimed to impress the viewer by creating a feeling of awe.

Gianlorenzo Bernini and the other artists who practiced the new Baroque style in art were determined to touch the emotions of the people looking at their paintings, sculptures, or buildings. The artists' work had to have a dramatic impact.

Baroque was the perfect style for the Roman Catholic Church of the time. In the 17th century, Catholic leaders were fighting back against the Protestant revolution in Christianity. The German priest Martin Luther had taken a stand against the authority of the Catholic Church in 1531, and from these roots Protestantism, a new strain of

turbed, complaining: "What the barbarians could not do, the Barberini did." Yet Bernini's design for the canopy became famous, and was often imitated in other Baroque churches.

In the 1630s, Bernini had an affair with Constanza Bonarelli, the wife of one of his assistants. He carved a beautiful portrait bust of his mistress in 1635. But four years later, Bernini

Christianity, grew. The Catholic Church wanted to remind people of its great power and wealth.

Artists found various ways to make their work more directly appealing and accessible to the world. Baroque painters often used dramatic effects of light and rich colors. Baroque sculptors like Bernini, meanwhile, chose dramatic subjects, and depicted them in a theatrical and emotional way.

The colonnade around St. Peter's Square in Rome (*above*) is a dazzling example of the Baroque style. It acts like a pair of giant arms, drawing in and overwhelming the audience.

married another woman, Caterina Tezio. He now became a devoted husband. He also became a devout Roman Catholic, the religion that he glorified in his art.

ECSTASY OF ST. THERESA

In the late 1640s, Bernini designed the work he considered to be his best, jokingly calling it his "least bad" piece.

The sculpture represents a religious vision experienced by the 16th-century Spanish saint, Theresa of Avila, in which she felt that she was pierced through the heart by an angel with a golden spear. She described it in her autobiography: "The pain was so great that I screamed aloud; but simultaneously I felt such infinite sweetness that I wished the pain to last eternally."

Bernini went to great lengths to represent this passion in his sculpture, known as the *Ecstasy of St. Theresa*, which stands in the church of Santa Maria della Vittoria. The saint's face reveals intense emotion, and her robes whirl about her swooning body to show her inner excitement. The figures are supported by "clouds" of marble.

A MAN OF MANY TALENTS

Bernini also painted for his own pleasure. His self-portraits are of such a high quality that they have sometimes been mistaken for works by the great Spanish artist, Velázquez (*see page 50*). He also loved the theater, and wrote dramas for which he designed and built the stage sets. He even composed music for an opera. The theater devices he used were often completely realistic, including floods and fire.

In 1644, Bernini met with failure for the first time. A crack appeared in the structure supporting the towers he had added to St. Peter's. This happened about the same time as his supporter Pope Urban died, and Bernini's enemies used it to get him dismissed as Rome's leading artistic director. The towers were demolished.

Fountain of the Four Rivers, 1648-51, by Gianlorenzo Bernini
This spectacular statue, situated in the Piazza Navona in Rome, is just one of many dramatic works that dominate Italy's capital. Bernini's impact on the city was immense.

Bernini's pride was hurt. He retreated to his studio, intending to make a dazzling new work to silence his critics. Yet it was not long before he was called back to work for the new pope, Innocent X. Innocent was extremely impressed by Bernini's design for a fountain for the Piazza Navona in Rome—the *Fountain of the Four Rivers*—and ordered its construction.

> "The only way not to risk executing Bernini's designs is not to see them."
> (Pope Innocent X)

The fountain was one of Bernini's finest achievements, and is a famous landmark in Rome to this day.

ST. PETER'S COLONNADE

Innocent's successor, Alexander VI, elected in 1655, also supported the artist and gave him two major projects. The first was a decorative sculpture surrounding the throne in St. Peter's that the saint himself was supposed to have used. And the second was for the colonnade around St. Peter's Square. It would be Bernini's greatest architectural achievement.

The artist himself described the sweeping arms of the colonnade as embracing Catholics "to reinforce their beliefs." Bernini wanted to overwhelm people coming to St. Peter's with awe and make them feel that they were arriving at the true center of the Roman Catholic faith.

In 1665, Bernini went on a foreign journey away from his beloved Rome. He had been invited to work for France's powerful king, Louis XIV. Louis, known as the "Sun King," kept a magnificent, extravagant court, and wanted Bernini to redesign the royal palace, the Louvre, in Paris.

The artist's fame arrived before him, and crowds lined the streets to greet him. The hopes of the French were not fulfilled, however. Louis did not approve Bernini's plan, and the artist returned home in 1666 after completing just one work, a bust of the king.

Bernini's later projects included palaces in Rome that inspired other Baroque buildings in Europe. He worked with great energy throughout his old age, remaining active as an artist until only a few months before his death, in 1680, at the age of 82.

MAJOR WORKS

1622-25	APOLLO AND DAPHNE
1624-33	BALDACCHINO IN ST. PETER'S, ROME
1635	BUST OF CONSTANZA BONARELLI
1645-52	ECSTASY OF ST. THERESA
1648-51	FOUNTAIN OF THE FOUR RIVERS
1656	COLONNADE OF ST. PETER'S SQUARE, ROME

43

ARTISTS

ANTHONY VAN DYCK

One of the most successful portraitists in the history of art, Van Dyck's stylish and sophisticated works set new standards of painting, and determined the course of English portraiture for the next two centuries.

Born in Antwerp on March 22, 1599, Anthony was the seventh child of Frans Van Dyck, a silk and linen merchant, and his wife, Maria Cuypers.

The boy showed artistic talent from an early age. In 1609, when he was ten years old, he was apprenticed to the painter Hendrick van Balen, who was an excellent teacher. Van Dyck continued to show great skill and in February 1618, when he was just 18, he was registered as a master by the Antwerp painters' guild.

THE EXAMPLE OF RUBENS

When Van Dyck was growing up, the artistic scene in Antwerp was dominated by Peter Paul Rubens (*see page 14*), a painter of enormous energy and inventiveness. Rubens greatly influenced Van Dyck's approach to life, as well as his artistic style.

In addition to being a great artist, Rubens was a respected diplomat—a man who was at ease in the most elevated social and intellectual circles. His example encouraged the young Van Dyck to adopt an aristocratic manner, and cultivate an image of himself as a man of sophistication and refinement.

WORKING WITH RUBENS

No one knows when the two artists first met, but Van Dyck was working for Rubens soon after being registered in the guild in 1618, perhaps even earlier. By 1620, he was recognized as Rubens's chief assistant. A contract for a series of works for an Antwerp church specifies that, while Rubens would produce the designs, the painting work would be done by "Van Dyck as well as some of his other pupils."

Despite Van Dyck's obvious talent and ambition, Rubens was too successful and self-confident to feel threatened by him. They admired each other and, seem always to have remained on good

Self-portrait, c.1630,
by Anthony Van Dyck
This elegant portrait shows the artist at the age of about 31.

44

terms. Still, Rubens may have encouraged Van Dyck to specialize in portraiture, the field he was least interested in himself, thus reducing the risk of rivalry.

Van Dyck's reputation soon spread outside his native Antwerp. In 1620, when the English countess of Arundel visited the city, her secretary wrote to the countess's husband, Thomas Howard, second earl of Arundel, about the young artist: "Van Dyck is still with Signor Rubens, and his works are hardly less esteemed than those of his master." Lord Arundel, as one of the most knowledgeable art collectors of his day, wanted to add this rising star to the distinguished list of artists he had already patronized.

PRESTIGIOUS PATRONS

In October 1620, Van Dyck duly arrived in London, where he began working for Arundel and for his wealthy rival, George Villiers, first duke of Buckingham. Van Dyck also received a generous payment from the king, James I, but it is not known what this was for.

Working for such influential patrons had other benefits. Van Dyck had access to the art collections of Arundel and Buckingham. These were particularly rich in pictures by the great Venetian painters, especially Titian, which filled Van Dyck with a desire to see Italy.

Van Dyck returned to Antwerp in March 1621, staying until October, when he left for Italy. He stayed there for the next six years, traveling widely—he went as far south as Sicily—but working mainly in Genoa, a port in the

GRACEFUL HANDS

The subtle movements and gestures of his sitters made Van Dyck's aristocratic clients come to life.

Van Dyck's many portraits are renowned for their grandeur and dignity. He created this impressiveness and beauty through a combination of many different elements, including the brilliantly detailed depiction of his wealthy sitters' rich costumes, and the sensitivity of his brushwork.

The client's pose could also help to add elegance to a painting. In many of his portraits, for example, Van Dyck shows his sitters with gracefully drooping hands (*above right*). These help to convey a sense of aristocratic bearing and casual ease.

A contemporary account of Van Dyck at work in his studio

northwest of Italy. There, he painted some masterful full-length portraits of members of the local nobility. In these, he moved away from the robust, monumental style of Rubens to one that was more elegant and refined. This new style was perfectly suited to depicting his aristocratic clients.

Van Dyck was entirely at home in the magnificent homes of his wealthy pa-

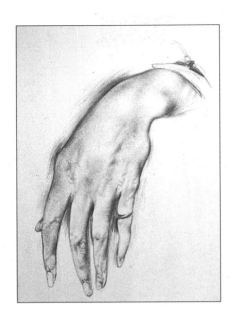

reveals that graceful hands were among the artist's favorite features. This evidence was left by a wealthy French banker and art collector, Everard Jabach, who had his portrait painted by Van Dyck. Jabach commented that the painter even took on models who had particularly attractive hands: "For the hands, he had in his employ people of both sexes who served him as models."

was mainly based in Antwerp. His work was much in demand. Yet he was still overshadowed by Rubens in his home country. In April 1632, he went back to England, where he was to spend most of the rest of his life.

WORKING FOR CHARLES I

Van Dyck's former patron, James I, had died in 1625, and been succeeded by his son, Charles I, who had a passionate love of painting. One of the greatest collectors of all time, he aimed to attract distinguished artists to work for him.

Charles already employed many painters. But Van Dyck was far more talented than any of them. Compared

> "No king ... has been imaged in such variety of genius." (20th-century art historian, Sir David Piper, on Van Dyck's portraits of Charles I)

trons, but his lordly manner did not always endear him to his fellow painters. On a visit to Rome, he upset other Flemish artists by refusing to join in the festivities with which they traditionally welcomed newcomers to the city.

Van Dyck's sister, Cornelia, died in Antwerp in September 1627, and he returned to the city to be with his family. For the next four-and-a-half years he

with his relaxed and elegant portraits, the work of his contemporaries looked stiff and old-fashioned. In July 1632, the king knighted Van Dyck and appointed him his chief court painter.

Van Dyck was well rewarded for his services. He was paid a good salary as well as extra money for special commissions. The king also gave him a house on the Thames River in London.

Charles I on Horseback with Seigneur de St. Antoine, 1633, by Anthony Van Dyck
This equestrian portrait presents the king as a powerful and dignified figure of majesty.

The house had a special landing stage so that the royal family could visit the painter more easily by sailing down the river from Whitehall Palace. In return, the artist immortalized the king in a series of striking portraits, showing Charles as a model of regal dignity. He also painted portraits of various members of the royal family and of numerous courtiers.

A COLORFUL LIFE

Van Dyck's private life was as colorful as his courtly surroundings. As his self-portraits show, he was handsome and debonair, and women evidently found him attractive. His name was romantically linked with a number of the women who posed for him. His official mistress was the fiery Margaret Lemon, described by a contemporary as "a demon of jealousy." Once, in a fit of rage, she tried to bite off Van Dyck's thumb to prevent him from painting again.

In spite of his success in England, Van Dyck was not entirely happy there. This was partly because he was valued almost entirely as a portraitist. He wanted a chance to show he could rival Rubens in history painting—impressive pictures of historical subjects.

SETTLING IN ENGLAND

In 1634-35, he visited Flanders, where he bought some land. It is likely that he intended returning permanently after Rubens's death, to take his place as the master's obvious successor. In 1639, however, he married Margaret Ruthven, a lady-in-waiting to the English queen, and again settled in England.

After Rubens died in May 1640, Van Dyck visited the Continent. In December, he traveled to the French capital, Paris, where he hoped to win a commission from Louis XIII to carry out decorations in the Louvre, the royal palace there. But Louis gave the job to the artist's great French contemporary, Nicolas Poussin (*see page 32*). Disappointed, Van Dyck returned to London.

FAILING HEALTH

In 1641, Van Dyck returned to the Continent. There, he fell ill, his frail health weakened by excessive work. By November, he was too weak to carry out a commissioned portrait in Paris. He arrived back in England a dying man.

On December 1, his wife gave birth to their only child, a daughter. Van Dyck died at his London home eight days later, aged 42, and was buried in the city's St. Paul's Cathedral—an unprecedented honor for a painter.

MAJOR WORKS

c.1620	CHRIST CROWNED WITH THORNS
1633	CHARLES I ON HORSEBACK WITH SEIGNEUR DE ST. ANTOINE
1633	QUEEN HENRIETTA MARIA
1635	CHARLES I IN THREE POSITIONS
1637	FIVE CHILDREN OF CHARLES I
c.1638	CUPID AND PSYCHE

DIEGO VELÁZQUEZ

Velázquez, who was painting masterpieces before his 20th birthday, excelled in all areas of painting, from historical to religious works. But it is for his portraits of the Spanish royal family and their court that he is best known.

Diego Velázquez was born in Seville, a city in southwest Spain, in 1599, probably a few days before his baptism on June 6. His parents were aristocrats, but they were comfortably off rather than rich.

LIFE IN SEVILLE

Seville was Spain's main port for trade with the Americas, which brought in a great deal of money. At the beginning of the 17th century, the city was a major artistic center and the most prosperous city in Spain. Studying there, the young Velázquez is said to have excelled at every subject he studied—but art was his first love.

In 1611, he was apprenticed to Francisco Pacheco, one of the leading artists in the city. Pacheco was a dull painter, but he was a cultivated man, whose house provided a stimulating atmosphere in which Velázquez could learn about art.

On March 14, 1617, at the age of 17, Velázquez graduated as a master painter.

A year later, on April 23, 1618, he married Pacheco's 15-year-old daughter Juana—proof of the high opinion his teacher had of him; Pacheco was impressed by the young artist's character and "the promise of his natural and great talent."

In time, Velázquez and his wife had two daughters, one of whom died in infancy. Beyond these facts, little is known of their domestic life. There is no known portrait of Juana by her husband, but it is likely that she was the model for some of his early paintings, such as *The Immaculate Conception* from around 1618.

IMPRESSING THE KING

Velázquez matured early as an artist, and soon established a reputation in Seville. But he had higher ambitions. In 1622, he visited the Spanish capital, Madrid,

Las Meninas (detail), 1656,
by Diego Velázquez
The proud Velázquez included himself in his masterpiece, poised at his easel.

home of the royal court, hoping to gain the attention of King Philip IV. Velázquez did not succeed at once, but the following year he was invited to return to Madrid by Philip's minister, the count-duke of Olivares. Olivares ordered the artist to paint a portrait of Philip. The picture impressed the king so much that he declared that from then on, no other artist should paint his portrait.

ROYAL HONORS

At the age of 24, Velázquez had suddenly become the most admired painter in Spain. He was attached to the court in Madrid for the rest of his life, and remained unchallenged as Philip's favorite artist.

> "A courtly gentleman of such great dignity as distinguishes any person of authority." (contemporary artist, Marco Boschini)

Philip admired Velázquez as a man as well as a painter, and he treated him with a friendliness that amazed contemporaries, for the Spanish court was a very formal place. "The liberality and affability with which Velázquez is treated by such a great monarch is unbelievable," wrote Pacheco. "He has a workshop in the king's gallery to which His Majesty has the key … so

AN EYE FOR TRUTH

Velázquez excelled in painting "low-life" scenes packed with carefully observed detail.

While still in his teens, Velázquez was painting works of great technical skill. Most of his early works were either religious paintings, or *bodegones*, a Spanish term referring to paintings of domestic scenes that feature still-life details.

His teacher, Pacheco, encouraged him to "go to nature for everything." Velázquez took this advice, bribing a local boy to act as his model, making numerous drawings of him in a variety of different poses. He was a careful observer of ordinary life.

An early example of Velázquez's *bodegones* is *Old Woman Cooking Eggs* of 1618, in which

that he can watch Velázquez paint at leisure, nearly every day."

The king appointed Velázquez to a series of important posts, such as Supervisor of the Works of the Palace. As a result, Velázquez spent a lot of time on court work instead of painting. He was well suited to his important role since he was dignified and had a natural air of authority.

every small detail is depicted with astonishing accuracy and precision (*above*).

Although such pictures were generally popular in Spain, some people criticized Velázquez for choosing such humble, low-life scenes to paint. But in all his work, the artist was more interested in capturing a sitter's essential character and humanity, than in their wealth, power, or social status.

Velázquez seems to have been a slow worker, and because so much of his time was taken up with court duties his output was small. He probably painted less than 200 paintings, of which 150 survive, which is an average of about one picture every two months.

After Velázquez settled in Madrid, in 1623, he became primarily a portraitist, depicting the king, the royal family, and various members of the court. He gave up painting *bodegones*, or domestic scenes, and only occasionally produced religious pictures. He also painted some historical and mythological pictures, and a pair of landscapes.

A NEW INFLUENCE

Velázquez came under many new influences. One of the most important of these was the colorful and passionate work of the 16th-century Venetian painter Titian; many of Titian's works were in the royal art collection.

Following the example of Titian and others, Velázquez began to pay less attention to detail in his pictures. Instead, he concentrated on the overall effect and atmosphere of a scene. He began to prefer bare settings, without the superbly painted still-life elements that had been such a feature of his earlier work in Seville.

At this time, the artist also changed the way he applied paint. He began to use the paintbrush with a lighter touch, and the strokes he made with it became broader and less well defined.

MEETING RUBENS

In 1629, Velázquez went to Italy and stayed for more than a year. Peter Paul Rubens (*see page 14*), the great Flemish painter, had encouraged Velázquez to go there. The two artists had become friends when Rubens visited Madrid in 1628. One contemporary states that Rubens "confessed that Velázquez was the greatest European painter."

Velázquez was inspired to see the great works of ancient and Renaissance

Old Woman Cooking Eggs, 1618, by Diego Velázquez
Velázquez painted this work only a year after completing his apprenticeship. It shows his skill in painting still life, and his early concern with capturing great detail.

art and in June 1629, he gained official permission from the king to visit Italy. He visited various major cities, spending about a year in Rome. From the masterpieces he saw, he learned how to draw the human body.

PAINTING THE COURT

After his return to Madrid in January 1631, Velázquez began a very productive period. He continued his pictures of the royal family, including a series of equestrian portraits—portraits in which the

sitter is posed on horseback. He also painted the court dwarfs and "fools" whom Philip, like other monarchs of the time, kept for his amusement. Velázquez portrayed each one with respect and sensitivity. His other work of the 1630s and 1640s included his finest religious paintings and *The Surrender of Breda*, showing the Dutch forces surrendering to the Spanish in 1625.

From 1648 to 1651, Velázquez made another lengthy visit to Italy, spending most of his time in Rome. There he painted a portrait of Pope Innocent X that was hailed at once as a great masterpiece. The pope himself thought that it had captured his character, saying that it was "too truthful." While he was in Rome, Velázquez had an affair with a widow who bore him a son, Antonio. No one knows what became of them, however.

> "One cannot understand [his work] if standing too close, but from a distance it is a miracle."
> (a contemporary)

MAJOR WORKS

1618	OLD WOMAN COOKING EGGS
c.1618	THE IMMACULATE CONCEPTION
c.1626	PORTRAIT OF PHILIP IV
1628-29	BACCHUS AND HIS COMPANIONS
1634-35	THE SURRENDER OF BREDA
c.1644	THE COURT FOOL SEBASTIAN DE MORRA
c.1648-51	THE ROKEBY VENUS
1650	PORTRAIT OF INNOCENT X
1656	LAS MENINAS (THE MAIDS OF HONOR)

In his final years, Velázquez continued to paint masterpieces, such as his famous picture of the Infanta Margareta Teresa and her ladies-in-waiting, *Las Meninas*, or The Maids of Honor. King Philip made him a Knight of Santiago in 1658, a title which had never been given to an artist before. The self-portrait in *Las Meninas* shows Velázquez proudly wearing the red cross of the order on his chest.

LATE STYLE

Las Meninas displays the artist's spontaneous and energetic technique that became increasingly loose in his later works. From a distance, every detail is clearly visible and intensely vivid; up close, the brushstrokes dissolve into a blur. The energy of his brushwork adds vivacity to this unconventional family portrait. In the self-portrait included in the painting, for example, the artist's hands are rendered by a few swift brushstrokes, and seem to move rapidly from palette to canvas.

A GREAT LOSS

On July 31, Velázquez took to his bed in his apartments in the royal palace, complaining of a fever. He died in Madrid on August 6, 1660, at the age of 61. He was "mourned by all," recorded contemporary artist Antonio Palomino, "and not least by the king." He was buried in the church of San Juan Bautisa. His grieving widow survived him by less than a week.

CLAUDE LORRAIN

One of the greatest landscape painters in the history of art, Claude had a dazzling ability to capture the subtle effects of changing light and weather on the countryside.

Claude Gellée was born at Chamagne in the Duchy of Lorraine, eastern France, in 1600. A version of the name of this region later replaced his own surname—and eventually he became so famous that he was referred to simply as Claude.

A HUMBLE CHILDHOOD

His childhood was obscure and his family was poor. Lorraine was famous for its pastry-making, and as a boy, Claude trained as a pastry cook. At the age of 13, he was settled in Italy and working in this way in Rome.

Claude was hired to work in the kitchens of the artist, Agostino Tassi. This was a piece of good luck since he later became Tassi's pupil and assistant. Tassi was known for his seascapes and landscapes, as well as for decorating several of the city's palaces. Claude may have worked with him on one project, the Villa Lante at Bagnaia.

As a young man, Claude also spent time in Naples, a seaport to the south of Rome. He worked alongside the Flemish landscape painter, Gottfried Wals. Claude loved the sweeping Gulf of Naples. He went on painting this part of the coast long after he had left there.

Apart from a brief return to Lorraine in 1625 to assist a local artist with some frescoes—a type of wall painting—Claude spent the rest of his life in Rome. He never married, although a daughter, Agnese, was born to him in 1653. His life seems to have been devoted to art.

CONTACT WITH POUSSIN

Claude lived in the artists' quarter in the northern part of Rome, where one of his neighbors was the painter Nicolas Poussin (*see page 32*). Many other artists from France and the Netherlands lived in the neighborhood, drawn there to study the classical art of Rome, and

Claude Lorrain
This undated portrait is an engraving of a French drawing. The name of the original artist is unknown.

CLAUDE LE LORRAIN.

the countryside, or Campagna, which surrounded the city.

Claude had a passionate interest in the works of Roman authors such as Virgil and Ovid. These writers often set their poems in an imaginary "golden age" of beautiful landscapes filled with shepherds and nymphs. Claude tried to create an equivalent in painting.

Claude worked on some frescoes in the Palazzo Crescenzi in Rome, in about 1630, but after that concentrated on producing smaller, portable pictures. He turned himself into the most important landscape painter in Rome.

A LOVE OF LANDSCAPE

His early patrons were unknown residents, but in about 1635, King Philip IV of Spain asked him to produce seven religious pictures to decorate the Buen Retiro Palace in Madrid. Claude now moved from making small, detailed works to a grand style, using sweeping landscapes. These pictures were more in keeping with the subjects he was now painting—stories from the Bible or from ancient Greek and Roman myths.

Like other visiting artists to Rome, Claude often went on sketching trips to the nearby countryside. He liked the wilder, picturesque places such as Tivoli, an area famous for its ruined temple, hills, and tumbling waterfalls.

Claude made study after study of trees, sheep, streams, and views. Very few of these, though, ever reappeared in his paintings, all of which were shaped by his imagination. He left out whatever would not fit in with the shape of the ideal landscape that he was

A FRAME FOR THE ACTION

Claude arranged the objects in his landscapes to draw the viewer into the picture.

To give a convincing impression of depth in his paintings, Claude often used a technique called *repoussoir*, from the French word meaning "to push back." He included towering tall trees or elegant classical buildings on either side of his scenes, stretching from the bottom almost to the top (*above right*). These help to push the viewer's attention deeper into the picture.

The trees or pieces of architecture are often painted dark and tall, standing out against a light expanse of sky. In this way, the sky and objects or people in the far distance are "pushed back."

creating—or anything that he decided was just too "real" or recognizable.

Claude's familiarity with the countryside enabled him to create light effects and the changing moods of nature—one of his great strengths. Claude often made up his landscapes in his head—yet they always look like a real piece of countryside. An example of this kind of poetic painting is *Landscape with*

Claude's technique means that, when you look at one of his paintings, your eye is drawn to the main action of the picture right away, even though the figures are often fairly small. Claude's carefully constructed scenes work almost like stage sets in a theater.

It is not only Claude's framing technique that creates depth in his work, but also his use of aerial perspective. This means that the farther your eye goes back, the lighter the colors become and the more hazy and faint the details. Claude's subtle lighting effects draw the eye very gradually to a distant horizon.

Psyche at the Palace of Cupid. Claude took his subject from the book *Metamorphoses* by the Roman poet Ovid, who lived from c.43 B.C. to 17 A.D. The picture, which shows Psyche—the human soul—outside the Palace of Amor, or love, has a fairytale quality.

Claude tended to organize his pictures in a certain way in order to create depth and structure. Trees usually occupy the foreground, positioned at the edges of the picture. In the middle ground, the main figures of the painting occur. Next, a winding path or stretch of water leads the viewer's eyes farther into the scene past another group of trees. In the distance, hills disappear in a bluish mist. A Claude landscape draws the viewers in, making them feel they could almost walk around in it.

LASTING INFLUENCE

Claude seemed to turn nature into a beautiful garden. His work had a great influence on later landscape painters, but it also played an important part in the English landscape movement of the 18th century. Aristocrats studied Claude's works with the aim of reproducing some of his effects on their land.

Wealthy people employed gardeners to replace their formal gardens with more naturally arranged ones that seemed to lead out into the countryside. They planted trees, dammed up streams, and built bridges and temples.

One immediate result of Claude's success was that he attracted forgers. In 1634, an artist called Sebastian Bourdon pretended that one of his own works was by Claude. To stop this from happening again, Claude began to draw copies of all his paintings in a book he called the *Liber Veritatis*, or "Book of Truth." He put in all necessary detail and often added the name of his patrons.

THE LATE WORKS

In the last 20 years of his life, Claude's paintings became more specialized. He had a small group of wealthy clients.

The Embarkation of St. Ursula, 1641, by Claude Lorrain
In the Christian legend, St. Ursula was a martyr of about the fourth century. In Claude's epic painting, St. Ursula watches some of her 11,000 companions as they board their ship after a pilgrimage to Rome. According to the story, all the pilgrims were massacred in Cologne, Germany. Claude painted this work for an Italian cardinal called Poli.

This was an episode taken from a Latin poem, the *Aeneid*, written by the Roman poet, Virgil, between 30 B.C. and 19 B.C. Aeneas, the hero of the poem, was the supposed founder of the Roman nation. Claude painted the work for Gasparo Altieri, and he included the Altieri family arms on Aeneas's ships.

For Duke Onofrio Colonna, Claude produced ten important paintings, including his last, *Ascanius Shooting the Stag of Silvia*. This was another scene from the *Aeneid*, in which Aeneas's son, Ascanius, provokes a war by killing a stag. As he neared the end of his life, Claude's pictures reflected a sad and thoughtful mood.

Claude died on November 23, 1682. He was buried in Santa Trinitá dei Monti, the church near the artists' quarter in Rome where he had lived.

MAJOR WORKS

1631	THE MILL
1641	THE EMBARKATION OF ST. URSULA
1644	LANDSCAPE WITH NARCISSUS AND ECHO
1648	SEAPORT WITH THE EMBARKATION OF THE QUEEN OF SHEBA; THE MARRIAGE OF ISAAC AND REBEKAH
1664	LANDSCAPE WITH PSYCHE AT THE PALACE OF CUPID
1675	LANDSCAPE WITH THE LANDING OF AENEAS AT PALLANTEUM

Often one of them would tell him what subject he wanted. As a result, Claude painted some subjects that no one else had ever tried, such as *Landscape with the Landing of Aeneas at Pallanteum*.

REMBRANDT VAN RIJN

The great Dutch artist, Rembrandt, made his name in portraiture, yet he excelled in every kind of subject and medium. Personal difficulties did not stop him from creating work that was both sensitive and powerful.

Born in Leiden, Holland, on July 15, 1606, Rembrandt Harmensz van Rijn was the eighth of a prosperous miller's nine children. Rembrandt was probably the most intelligent of the family. He went to Leiden's Latin school, whereas the other children learned trades. He may also have attended the town's university, but by the time he was 14, he had probably already started his apprenticeship as a painter.

AN ARTISTIC TRAINING

Rembrandt trained with several painters. Pieter Lastman, one of the leading Dutch artists of the time, was the only one who had any significant effect on his style. Rembrandt studied with Lastman in Amsterdam in about 1624. Lastman specialized in small-scale mythological and historical scenes. His lively works, full of vivid gestures and expressions, strongly influenced the young Rembrandt.

By 1625, Rembrandt had returned to Leiden, where he set up as an independent artist. He was only 19. He became friends with another promising Leiden painter, Jan Lievens, with whom he probably shared a studio for a while. Soon, a great future was being predicted for the two young men.

MAKING A NAME

Late in 1631 or early in 1632, Rembrandt moved to Amsterdam, which was to be his home for the rest of his life. Amsterdam was the most important city in the country, and a great center of international trade. Here, over the next few years, Rembrandt's career went from strength to strength, mainly through his portraits of merchants and other prosperous citizens.

There were other good portraitists in the city at the time, but Rembrandt easily matched them in delicacy and subtlety of painting costume, and

Self-portrait, 1657, by Rembrandt van Rijn
Rembrandt painted many self-portraits. This sensitive and thoughtful painting shows the artist at the age of 51.

glossiness of finish—and far surpassed them in capturing a vibrant sense of life and personality.

A HAPPY MARRIAGE

Rembrandt prospered in his personal as well as his professional life. In 1634, when he was 28, he married Saskia van Uylenburgh, the wealthy 21-year-old cousin of a picture-dealer friend. There are no contemporary accounts of their married life, but they are hardly necessary, for it is obvious from Rembrandt's many paintings, drawings, and etchings of Saskia that he adored her.

But there was sadness in their life together. Between 1635 and 1641, Saskia had four children, only one of whom—their son Titus—lived longer than two months. Saskia had always been frail, and died in 1642.

THE NIGHT WATCH

This was a pivotal year in Rembrandt's life, for it also marked the completion of his largest and most famous painting, known as *The Night Watch*. This shows a band of "civic guards"—ordinary citizens who trained as soldiers, ready to fight in a national emergency. The title is misleading, since the picture actually depicts the guard marching out in daylight—as cleaning in 1946-47 revealed.

This painting was revolutionary in its approach to group portraiture. The Dutch had a strong tradition of group portraits, which usually concentrated on depicting each member of a group—such as a town council or a committee—in as realistic a way as possible. Usually, sitters would pay to be in-

---

REMBRANDT'S ENGRAVINGS

The greatest master of etching, Rembrandt made full use of the spontaneity the medium allows.

Etching is a method of engraving in which the design is bitten into a polished metal plate—usually copper—with acid. The plate is first coated with an acid-resistant substance, or "ground." The etcher then draws a design upon the grounded plate with a steel etching needle, allowing the point to cut through the dark ground and expose the metal beneath. The artist then immerses the plate in a bath of acid, which bites into the metal wherever the ground has been pierced by the needle. Darker effects can be created by immersing the plate again, so that the acid bites more deeply.

---

cluded in a painting; the more money they paid, the more prominently they would appear.

By contrast, Rembrandt concentrated on creating a dramatic scene rather than showing each of the sitters in detail. He focused on making the event as exciting as he could, using vivid colors and theatrical lighting, with dramatic contrasts of light and dark.

Rembrandt brought a new immediacy, vigor, and power to the technique. He used a variety of etching tools to create different effects. At times, Rembrandt used the etching needle as fluently as if it were a pen. At others, he reworked the copper plate again and again to produce a velvety black richness in the finished print.

In one of his most dramatic and atmospheric religious etchings, *The Three Crosses* (*above*), light seems to pour down on the scene of Christ's crucifixion from Heaven.

fact, admire the painting. One contemporary artist, for example, felt that it made the paintings hanging next to it seem "like playing cards."

From about this time, however, Rembrandt's career started to go downhill in worldly terms. He painted fewer commissioned portraits and more religious subjects, seeming to work more to please himself than to paint what potential buyers wanted. His pictures became more inward-looking and spiritual.

His technique changed too, moving away from the careful detail of his early works toward a much broader style in

---

"It is so painter-like in thought, so dashing in movement, and so powerful ...."
(artist, Samuel van Hoogstraten, on *The Night Watch*)

Captain Banning Cocq and his lieutenant, for example, are highlighted by a shaft of light which falls from the top left of the painting. The captain seems about to step out from the canvas.

According to legend, the guardsmen it represented hated *The Night Watch* because it did not show each of them clearly. The little evidence that survives, however, suggests that people did, in

which he applied paint with rich, vigorous brushstrokes. In the 1650s and 1660s, his *impasto*—thickly applied paint—was one of the most remarkable features of his work.

After Saskia's death, Rembrandt hired a widow called Geertge Dircx as a nurse for Titus. She and Rembrandt became lovers, but a few years later he rejected her for a servant called Hendrickje Stoffels. Hendrickje stayed

The Night Watch, 1642, by Rembrandt van Rijn
This painting shows the militia company of Captain Banning Cocq. The captain—in black with red sash—orders his lieutenant, van Ruytenburch—in yellow—to march the company out. The work shows Rembrandt's great ability to create drama in an ordinary event.

with Rembrandt for the rest of her life, and they had two children. The first died soon after birth, but the second—a daughter named Cornelia, born in 1654—was the only one of Rembrandt's six children to survive him.

FALLING INTO DEBT

During his successful early years, Rembrandt had been extravagant. He lived in a large and splendid house, and collected art on a grand scale. But in the 1650s, the Dutch economy went into a severe decline because of war with England. The artist—no longer earning a fortune as a portraitist—found himself getting deeper and deeper into financial trouble.

Things came to a head in 1656 when Rembrandt was unable to pay his debts. He managed to avoid bankruptcy—for which he could have been imprisoned—

by convincing the authorities that he had acted honorably in all of his business dealings.

Rembrandt was forced to sell his beloved art collection and move to a much smaller house in a poorer part of the city. Hendrickje and Titus found a

> "In the last years of his life, he worked so fast that his pictures, when examined close by, looked as if they had been daubed with a bricklayer's trowel." (Dutch art historian, Arnold Houbraken)

way to help him financially by forming a small picture-dealing company, with Rembrandt technically their employee. This meant that he was protected from his creditors.

A GREAT LEGACY

Houbraken recorded that "in the autumn of his life [Rembrandt] kept company mainly with common people and such as practiced art." Yet Rembrandt remained a respected figure in the art world, and still received important commissions.

Hendrickje died in 1663, and Titus five years later, but as far as his self-portraits reveal, Rembrandt faced his hardships with dignity and no trace of bitterness. His work continued to grow in freedom of technique and depth of expression to the very end of his life; his late masterpieces include some of the most moving pictures ever painted.

Rembrandt died on October 4, 1669, aged 63. He was buried four days later in Amsterdam, leaving behind a legacy of some 500 paintings, 300 etchings, and 1,000 drawings.

A LASTING REPUTATION

Rembrandt remained an admired artist throughout the 18th century, but there was a feeling among many critics that he had wasted his talent on lowly subjects. His reputation rose in the 19th century with the Romantic movement, which brought with it the idea that an artist should ignore fashion, and express his innermost feelings. By the end of the century, he was generally regarded as one of the greatest of all painters.

MAJOR WORKS

1632	THE ANATOMY LESSON OF DR. TULP
1635	SELF-PORTRAIT WITH SASKIA
1642	THE NIGHT WATCH
1654	PORTRAIT OF JAN SIX
1654	BATHSHEBA
1655	WOMAN BATHING
c.1665	THE JEWISH BRIDE

JAN VERMEER

Vermeer's pictures are among the most famous and best-loved images in the history of art, yet little is known of his life. He produced only a handful of works, but they raised Dutch painting of everyday life to new heights.

Johannes, or Jan, Vermeer was born in October 1632 in Delft, a town in the Dutch Republic, which is now part of Holland. He was the second of two children. His father, Reynier, had been a silkworker, but in 1641 he gave his job up to buy an inn in the main square of Delft.

LIFE IN DELFT

In Vermeer's day, Delft was the fourth largest town in the country. Its citizens were well-off. People came from all over Europe to buy the pottery made in Delft. Vermeer rarely left the town, and probably spent his whole life there.

It is likely that he trained in Delft, too. As well as running the inn, his father was also a part-time art dealer. With his excellent connections in the town's art world, it would have been easy to find an art teacher for his son.

Vermeer may have worked under Carel Fabritius, who had settled in Delft in about 1650, after studying with Rembrandt van Rijn (*see page 62*).

Fabritius was an outstandingly talented artist, but his short career ended tragically when he died in a gunpowder explosion in 1654; he was only 32 years old. Vermeer owned three of Fabritius's paintings, and there were some similarities in their work.

In 1653, Vermeer was made a master in Delft's guild of artists. In the same year, he married Catharina Bolnes. Catharina came from a higher social class than Vermeer's. Her mother, who was divorced and wealthy, disapproved of the match at first. But she later gave her consent, and supported the couple after their wedding. Very little is known of the marriage, except that the couple had 15 children together, 11 of whom survived. It is also likely that Vermeer used his wife as a model for some of his pictures, and that the artist converted to his wife's Catholic faith.

The Painter in his Studio, c.1666,
by Jan Vermeer
It is suggested that Vermeer has shown himself here in a teasing self-portrait.

Maid with a Milk Jug, c.1658-60, by Jan Vermeer
This painting shows a girl in a typical Dutch house. Little details, such as the Delft pottery tiles along the baseboard and the footwarmer on the floor, add to realism of the scene.

little raised points of paint that suggest the play of light on objects.

The *Maid with a Milk Jug* shows a girl quietly absorbed in her task. The colors are fresh and cool, and the image is one of composed peace and harmony. The specks of light on the surface are like those that would appear through an unfocused lens. This suggests that Vermeer used an optical device called a camera obscura when working.

RESPECT AND SUCCESS

By the early 1660s, Vermeer was a respected figure in Delft. In 1662, at an exceptionally young age, he was made a "hooftman," or headman, of the town painters' guild. At the same time, his paintings were selling well. They were either bought by the local officials of Delft, or given to tradesmen to clear debts. Vermeer may also have had a regular patron, Jacob Dissius. In 1682, seven years after Vermeer's death, he owned 19 of the artist's paintings.

In spite of this patronage, Vermeer found himself in severe financial difficulties. In 1657, he had to borrow

---

"His paint looks like crushed pearls melted together." (17th-century Dutch painter and art critic, Jan Veth)

---

a large sum of money, and in 1672, he rented out his house and moved in with his mother-in-law.

Toward the end of his life, his style became harder and lost its freshness. Vermeer was such a marvelous craftsman that every single picture he painted contained touches of great beauty. But as his financial problems worsened, his paintings seemed to lack the naturalness of his earlier works.

When the Dutch Republic was invaded by the French in 1672, an economic crisis caused the Dutch art market to collapse. Vermeer's already unstable business collapsed with it.

When he died in 1675, at the age of 43, Vermeer left a large debt and a family of young children. A month after his funeral, his widow sold two of his paintings to a baker to settle her debt with him. Soon afterward, she was declared bankrupt.

A FORGOTTEN MASTER

Vermeer's paintings had sold for high prices in his lifetime, and they continued to be admired after his death. But after a while, his name virtually disappeared from history. His pictures were often sold at auctions wrongly attributed to other Dutch artists.

It was not until the 19th century that his name was rescued from oblivion by the French journalist, Théophile Thoré, who identified about two-thirds of the Vermeer paintings we know today. After this, Vermeer's fame grew quickly, and his works are now among the most highly prized possessions in the world's greatest galleries.

MAJOR WORKS

c.1658-60	THE GLASS OF WINE; SOLDIER WITH LAUGHING GIRL; MAID WITH A MILK JUG
c.1660	THE LITTLE STREET; VIEW OF DELFT
c.1660-65	THE MUSIC LESSON; THE CONCERT
c.1666	THE PAINTER IN HIS STUDIO
1670	THE LACEMAKER; THE LOVE LETTER

WILLIAM SHAKESPEARE

Probably the most famous writer of all time, William Shakespeare produced a dazzling collection of plays, as well as an elegant series of poems, that still enchant audiences all around the world to this day.

William Shakespeare's life began in the market town of Stratford-upon-Avon in central England. There is no record of his birth. But a boy of the same name was baptized at Holy Trinity Church in Stratford on April 26, 1564.

William's father was a successful glovemaker and leather craftsman. He also dealt in timber, grain, and other products, and owned several houses in Stratford. At one time, he was the town's mayor, and he held many other public positions during his lifetime.

It seems likely that Shakespeare, as the son of a well-off citizen, went to Stratford grammar school. He did not go to a university, however. Many writers then were highly educated in the literature of ancient Rome and Greece. In comparison, Shakespeare probably knew little Latin and even less Greek. By today's standards, however, he was still well read in the classics.

In 1582, William married Anne Hathaway, a landowner's daughter. He was aged 18, and Anne was eight years older. The following year Anne gave birth to a girl, Susanna. In 1585, twins—Hamnet and Judith—were born.

THEATRICAL BEGINNINGS

Nobody knows what happened to Shakespeare for the next few years. He may have been a schoolteacher in Stratford for a while. Somehow, he became involved in the theater. In 1587, the Queen's Men, a group of actors from London, arrived in Stratford. But shortly before the actors' arrival, one of them had been killed, leaving them one person short for their performances. Some people suggest that Shakespeare replaced the missing actor.

Whether or not this is true, by 1592, Shakespeare was a successful actor and playwright in London, probably writing plays for the group with which he acted.

Portrait of a man, by Nicholas Hilliard
This miniature, thought to show William Shakespeare, was painted by one of the most famous 16th-century English artists.

His reputation had grown so much that a jealous rival playwright published a pamphlet attacking him.

By this time, Shakespeare had written his first history plays, the three parts of *Henry VI*. These were great successes and inspired him to produce the comedies *Love's Labour's Lost* and *The Comedy of Errors*. He also wrote *Richard III*, another history play. Its

---

"To be, or not to be: that is the question: Whether 'tis nobler ... to suffer ... or to take arms against a sea of troubles...."
(Hamlet)

---

main character, King Richard III of England, was the first of many fascinating, complicated villains in Shakespeare's works.

WORKING METHODS

We do not know when many of Shakespeare's plays were written or first performed. This is mainly because of the way theaters worked at the time. Plays were performed six days a week, a different one each afternoon since the audience wanted new plays all the time. The most popular ones were repeated, but in a year, a company would put on around 40 different plays. As many as 20 of these would be new.

THE TRAGEDY OF HAMLET

When he wrote *Hamlet*, Shakespeare created one of the most famous plays in the English language.

Hamlet is the tragic story of Prince Hamlet of Denmark (*right*), probably Shakespeare's best-known character. At the start of the play, Hamlet's father, the king, dies. His uncle, Claudius, seizes the throne and marries Hamlet's mother. The prince then sees a vision of his father's ghost, which tells him that the villainous Claudius had murdered his father. The ghost urges Hamlet to seek revenge.

Hamlet thinks long and hard about the difficult situation he finds himself in. But he is very bad at making up his mind. He is torn between duty to his mother and wanting revenge for

With such great demand, playwrights had to work fast. They took the inspiration for their stories from many different sources—books of English history, folktales, accounts of the Roman Empire, or ancient Greek and Roman literature. Most writers followed established rules and fashions, rather than create new ones, and Shakespeare was no different. His dramas had to

his father's murder. He cannot decide which is the most noble course of action. Most of the things that happen to him occur almost by accident.

In the end, Hamlet kills Claudius, but not before he himself is injured in a sword fight. He dies immediately afterward.

please a wide audience. Like many playwrights at the time he wrote in "blank verse"—poetry with a strong, regular rhythm but without rhymes.

A CHANGE OF DIRECTION

In June 1592, Shakespeare's early success in the theater came to an abrupt end. The highly infectious "Black Death," or bubonic plague, was killing thousands of Londoners. As part of an attempt to halt the spread of the disease, the city's theaters closed down. For two years, Shakespeare could not act or produce any plays.

During this enforced absence from the stage, Shakespeare turned to writing poetry instead. He completed two long poems based on ancient Greek and Roman myths. He may also have begun writing his sonnets, a series of poems, each 14 lines long. Many of his sonnets describe the intense emotions of being in love. They concern the personal entanglements of a nobleman, a mysterious "dark lady," and a third person who may be the author himself. Shakespeare probably intended these poems for circulation among a small group of friends, and might have preferred them to be kept private. But in 1609 they were published.

A PROSPEROUS CAREER

In June 1594, the London theaters were allowed to reopen at last. Shakespeare teamed up with the Lord Chamberlain's Men, one of London's leading acting groups. Once again, he worked as an actor as well as producing some of his most popular plays. Around this time, he wrote a comical fantasy— *A Midsummer Night's Dream*—and a love story, *Romeo and Juliet*, which was the tale of two young lovers whose affair is destined to end in tragedy.

The Lord Chamberlain's Men were very successful, and Shakespeare, who had a financial share in the group, made a great deal of money. The company was so famous and popular that it

Romeo beneath Juliet's balcony, engraving after Frank Dicksee
**Shakespeare's tale of a tragic, young couple is the most famous love
story of all time. One night, Romeo climbs into Juliet's garden and
sees her on her balcony: "It is my lady; O, it is my love!" he gasps.**

received the honor of an invitation to
perform in Queen Elizabeth I's
luxurious palace during Christmas 1594.

Two years later, however, tragedy
struck Shakespeare's life, when his 11-
year-old son, Hamnet, died. Perhaps this
made Shakespeare think more of his
family and want to spend more time at
home in Stratford. The following year,
he invested some of his theatrical
earnings in a splendid house, called
New Place, in the town.

But between 1598 and 1600, he was
back in London to produce his
comedies *As You Like It*, *Twelfth
Night*, and *Much Ado About Nothing*.

These works contain many familiar features from traditional English stage comedies. Their stories include plots of disguise and mistaken identity, funny dances, and humorous songs.

Between 1600 and 1606, Shakespeare produced his four greatest tragedies: *Hamlet, Othello, King Lear,* and *Macbeth.* Each play takes its title from its central character, whose good qualities are spoiled by a failing in his

> "William Shakespeare is the applause, delight, the wonder of our Stage."
> (17th-century writer, Ben Jonson)

personality, or by the situation in which he finds himself. Othello, for example, has only one failing—his jealousy—but this causes him to murder his wife. Macbeth's ambition drives him to commit a string of evil acts. Hamlet is a prince who must avenge his father's murder, even though by doing so he dooms himself to die. All four plays contain passages of unforgettable poetry, absorbing plots, and subtle yet powerful drama.

THE END OF THE MAGIC

Toward the end of his career, Shakespeare wrote a series of dramas often known as his "late plays." These turn away from the pain and darkness of the tragedies toward happy, positive themes—for instance, the reuniting of long-separated family members.

Shakespeare's last play, *The Tempest,* contains a scene in which a magician, near the end of his life, gives up his trusted magic spells. Some people see this as the playwright's final goodbye—the moment when he signed off after years of theatrical magic.

AN ENDURING GENIUS

In 1610, at the age of 46, William Shakespeare retired from London to Stratford. He died on April 23, 1616, and was buried in his hometown. Seven years later, his collected plays were published in one edition for the first time. Already, some people believed that he had lasting stature as a writer. As his friend, the contemporary playwright Ben Jonson, wrote of Shakespeare: "He was not of an age, but for all time."

MAJOR WORKS

1591-92	HENRY VI, PARTS 1–3
1593	RICHARD III
1593-95	THE TAMING OF THE SHREW
c.1595	ROMEO AND JULIET
1595-99	MUCH ADO ABOUT NOTHING; TWELFTH NIGHT; A MIDSUMMER NIGHT'S DREAM
c.1600-6	HAMLET; OTHELLO; KING LEAR; MACBETH
1610-11	THE TEMPEST

JOHN DONNE

In his own lifetime, John Donne was more famous for his religious preaching than his poetry. Most of his poems were published only after his death, and his genius was not widely recognized until the 20th century.

John Donne was born in London in 1572. He came from a distinguished and well-connected family. His father was the head of the local ironmongers and his mother was the daughter of a famous playwright. But despite their excellent connections, the Donnes suffered terrible persecution because of their Roman Catholic faith.

A TURBULENT CHILDHOOD

It was a dangerous time to be a Roman Catholic in England. In 1533, King Henry VIII had rejected the Roman Catholic Church when the pope would not grant him a divorce. Furious at this, Henry created the Church of England, and made it illegal to be a Catholic. For the next 100 years, religion was the cause of many deadly quarrels both at home and in Europe. England was often at war with Spain, a Catholic country.

Donne's family knew all about this. His grandfather had been forced to flee England, and one of his uncles had been tried for treason; in both cases, their only crime was that they were Catholic. John's brother, Henry, was flung into jail in 1593 because he had given refuge to a Catholic priest. He died in prison.

Under such conditions, John's childhood was spent in an atmosphere of secrecy and fear. This had a great effect on him. For many years he remained a Catholic, but later in life he would join the Church of England.

John became a student at Hart Hall, Oxford, in 1584. He stayed there for three years. Then he probably continued his studies at Cambridge, followed by travels overseas. In 1592, he enrolled to study law in London. Soon he was visiting the city's theaters, where he probably saw some of William Shakespeare's (*see page 74*) first plays being performed.

Donne himself was busy both trying to get a job, and writing poetry. Many

John Donne, c. 1610, by Isaac Oliver
This portrait shows the writer, probably in his late 30s, wearing a fashionable stand-up collar, or ruff.

JOHN MILTON

Milton devoted his life to his two passions: poetry and politics. Having played a part in one of England's most turbulent periods, he set to work on an epic poem which was to become a landmark in Western literature.

John Milton was born in London, on December 9, 1608. His father was a "scrivener"—someone who writes legal documents. He made a very good living, and paid for his son to have a first-rate education. John had a private tutor at home until he was around 12 years old, when he went to St. Paul's School in London.

A DIVIDED CHURCH

Milton's family were members of the Church of England. Many people at the time were calling for changes in the Church. The reformers felt that it was too similar to the Roman Catholic Church, particularly because its bishops had great power over the priests and the ordinary worshippers. John must have learned all about these arguments from his first tutor, Thomas Young, who was a member of the Presbyterians— a Scottish group of church reformers.

In 1624, Milton went to study at Christ's College, Cambridge. He was there for seven years and wrote many poems, not only in English but also in Latin and Italian. He was a very serious student and did not have many friends. His nickname was "the lady of Christ's," perhaps because he did not take part in the other students' fun and games.

When he left the university in 1631, Milton wanted to become a minister in the Church of England. But he felt that he needed to learn more before he started preaching. He spent the next five years studying privately in London.

Milton read widely, and thought about the arguments between the defenders of the Church of England and those who wanted to reform. The reformers wanted simpler church services and a purer form of worship that focused on each individual person's relationship with God. Because they wanted to purify the Church, they were called "Puritans." John found he

John Milton, 1670, by William Faithorne **This portrait of Milton illustrated the frontispiece to one of the early editions of the writer's great epic poem,** *Paradise Lost.*

A. Faithorne ad Vivum   Delin. et sculpsit

Ioannis Miltoni Effigies Ætat: 62
1670.

Scene from **Paradise Lost,** *c.1810, by William Blake*
Milton's masterpiece inspired generations of writers and artists, including Blake, a 19th-English century poet, philosopher, and artist.

agreed with the Puritans more and more. He chose not to become a Church of England minister after all.

Instead, he decided to spend his life writing. In 1634, he wrote a musical drama called *Comus*. In 1637, both his mother and a friend from his university died. The following year, he expressed his grief by writing a powerful elegy— a sorrowful song—called "Lycidas."

Soon afterward, Milton traveled to France and then Italy, which he loved. In the summer of 1639, news of trouble back in London prompted him to return.

Charles I, the king of England, was trying to stop the reforms of the Puritans. When members of Parliament voiced their support of the Puritans, Charles clashed with Parliament. The hostility between the king's supporters

—the Royalists—and the supporters of Parliament—the Parliamentarians—grew, and in 1642, civil war erupted. Milton backed the Parliamentarians.

A DISASTROUS MARRIAGE

That year, Milton, then 33, married a 17-year-old girl called Mary Powell. The match was a complete disaster. After just six weeks, Mary left him. Milton was upset, and responded by writing pamphlets on divorce. At the time, a married couple could only divorce if one of them had committed adultery. Milton argued that couples should be allowed to divorce if they could not get on. Many people laughed at the idea.

Undeterred, Milton continued with his political writing. In 1643, he wrote a defense of free speech. Mary returned in 1644, and had three daughters with John before she died in 1652. In 1646, Milton published *Poems*, a collection of all the poetry he had written.

A POLITICAL CAREER

In 1649, the Parliamentarians, led by Oliver Cromwell, defeated the Royalists, and executed King Charles. Cromwell formed a new government, and gave Milton the job of translating diplomatic papers and defending the government against its critics. Then, in 1652, after years of poring over books, often in poor light, Milton went blind.

In 1656, he married Katherine Woodcock. She died just two years later, in 1658. In the same year, Cromwell died. He had been such a strong leader that no one could replace him. By 1660, England had a king again—Charles II.

This marked the end of Milton's political career. Yet he still had ambitions as a poet. For years, he had been planning a great epic—a long poem that tells a heroic story. He chose the tale of Adam and Eve from the Old Testament, which tells how God threw Adam and Eve out of Paradise because they disobeyed him. Milton called his poem *Paradise Lost*.

Since he was blind, Milton could not write his poetry down. Each day he dictated a section of up to 40 lines. One of his daughters, a secretary, or a friend would transcribe the words. It took four years to complete the 12-book-long poem. When it was published in 1667, some people immediately recognized it as a work of genius—although many were baffled by it.

Milton had achieved his ambition and become a great poet. He wrote two more epic works—*Paradise Regained* and *Samson Agonistes*—before he died in London on November 8, 1674.

MAJOR WORKS

1620s	L'ALLEGRO; IL PENSEROSO
1634	COMUS
1638	LYCIDAS
1641-42	FIRST POLITICAL WORKS
1643	AREOPAGITICA
1646	POEMS
1667	PARADISE LOST
1671	PARADISE REGAINED; SAMSON AGONISTES

CLAUDIO MONTEVERDI

The Italian composer is best-known today for his madrigals—musical settings of poems, usually about love—and his operas, which he brought to life with his great gift for dramatic, emotional music.

Claudio Monteverdi was born in Cremona, a small town in northern Italy, on May 15, 1567. His father ran a shop close to Cremona Cathedral, where Claudio was able to study music under the choirmaster, Marc Antonio Ingegneri. He was a brilliant pupil, and published his first book of compositions at the age of 15. In the next five years, three more books were published under his name.

WORKING IN MANTUA

Cremona offered little work for musicians, so in 1591 Monteverdi moved to the nearby city of Mantua. There he found a job as a violinist for the aristocratic Gonzaga family. The court of the Gonzagas was very cultured and was full of great artists, poets, and musicians. Duke Vincenzo Gonzaga, Monteverdi's employer, was especially fond of music.

In the early part of his career, Monteverdi achieved great success with his madrigals. They were "polyphonic"—each member of a small group would sing a different melody line, every one of which had to harmonize with all the others. Strict rules governed which kinds of harmony were allowed.

MUSIC OF EMOTION

Monteverdi's early work was fairly conventional, but upon meeting the most important musician at the Gonzagas' court, he changed his approach entirely. Giaches de Wert believed that music should match exactly the emotion of the words it was set to—even if that meant disregarding the rules of harmony.

Starting with a book published in 1592, Monteverdi began to revolutionize the madrigal. The more voices a composer used, the more care he had to take that they all harmonized.

Claudio Monteverdi, by Domenico Feti
The Italian painter Feti was a contemporary of the composer. The date of this portrait is unknown.